Meditations from the Cross

Good Friday at Luther Memorial Church

Brad Pohlman, Editor

© 2013 Brad C. Pohlman

All rights reserved.

Published in the United States of America by Luther Memorial Church Publishing. All rights reserved. No portion of this book may be used, reproduced, or transmitted, in any manner whatsoever without written permission from the publisher, except for brief excerpts used in critical articles and reviews.

ISBN 978-0-578-13050-7

Unless otherwise noted, scripture quotations are taken from The New Revised Standard Version of the Bible, © 1989, by the Division of Christian Education of the National Council of Churches of Christ in the United States of America.

Used by permission.

Cover design: Robin Wagner
Cover photo: Processional Cross from Luther Memorial

Printed in the United States of America

Luther Memorial Church
1021 University Avenue
Madison, Wisconsin 53715
608-258-3160
www.luthermem.org

Contents

Preface

Father, forgive them; for they know not what they do.
Writing and erasing	Jon Enslin
Black marker	Twink Jan-McMahon
Preemptive	Larry Thies

Today you will be with me in paradise.
Being with Jesus	Larry Thies
Through Baptism	Amy Grunewald Mattison
Eden restored	Franklin Wilson

Woman, behold your son! Behold your mother.
God-bearer	Jon Enslin
Your heart's home	John Ruppenthal
A mother's love	Peter Shervin

My God, my God, why have you forsaken me.
Not the God we want	Larry Thies
Journey by night	Jim Koza
Alone	John Ruppenthal

I thirst.
Melody and meaning	Franklin Wilson
Treading our path	Amy Johnson
Sour	Sherri Frederickson
Looking up	Daniel Ruge

It is finished.
Fruition	John Ruppenthal
Resistance	Cindy Crane
Completion	Franklin Wilson

Father, into your hands I commend my spirit.
A Broad place	Amy Grunewald Mattison
A way to die	Larry Thies
Last words	Franklin Wilson

Preface

For more than three decades, Luther Memorial Church has offered a *Tre Ore* service from Noon to 3 PM on Good Friday. The service commemorates the passion and death of Jesus and includes periods of extensive silence, psalmody, hymns and short meditations on the seven last words of Christ from the Gospels.

This book is a result of the generosity of the people of Luther Memorial Church in providing me a sabbatical in the summer of 2013. One of my sabbatical projects is this book—a collection of twenty-two meditations that were preached on Good Friday at Luther Memorial during the period 2008-2013. All the preachers in this series are, or were at the time of their preaching, participants in the life and ministry of Luther Memorial. To them, I offer my thanks and gratitude. I am thankful to my colleagues for their insight and wisdom in their preaching, in their fidelity to the gospel, and the gift of their ministry in this place.

I also wish to thank my colleague in ministry, Franklin Wilson, for reading a draft of this collection; to Neal Deunk who proofed the text; to Robin Wagner who designed the cover, and to Connie Lavine who provided generous financial support.

To you the reader, I hope that you will read and meditate on the words written in this book. And that you may see, as one of our preachers put it, "What happens before three o'clock, and what happens after it is finished, changes everything." Our commemoration of the passion and death of Jesus is meant for us to see that it really is a "Good" Friday. Looking back from an empty tomb, to a man on a cross, we see salvation worked for us, for the world, and for all creation.

Rev. Brad C. Pohlman
Holy Cross Day
September 14, 2013

The First Word from the Cross

Two others also, who were criminals, were led away to be put to death with him. When they came to the place that is called The Skull, they crucified Jesus there with the criminals, one on his right and one on his left. Then Jesus said, "Father, forgive them; for they do not know what they are doing." And they cast lots to divide his clothing. And the people stood by, watching; but the leaders scoffed at him, saying, "He saved others; let him save himself if he is the Messiah of God, his chosen one!" The soldiers also mocked him, coming up and offering him sour wine, and saying, "If you are the King of the Jews, save yourself!" Luke 23:32-37

Prayer

Lord Jesus, we take a deep breath and prepare to stare at your bleeding body for three hours. We warn you, O God, that we are the kind of people who don't know the difference between our enemy and our savior. Let your Son come close to us, and prepare to pay the price for our ignorance and cruelty. But do, we pray, let him come close to us, now and always. Amen.

Writing and erasing

My entire ministry I have understood these words, "Father forgive them, for they do not know what they are doing," as applying directly to the situation—Jesus asking the Father to forgive those who unjustly caused him such great pain and suffering. It has conjured up a series of delicious self-righteous images for me. Imagine you are the soldier who spit on Jesus, or the one who forced the crown of thorns on his head. Or imagine that you are Pilate who chose not to do justice but to humiliate those accursed and troublesome Jews. Or imagine you are the high priest in whose home Jesus was judged and imprisoned. You have died. Now you stand before the very same person you have caused to suffer pain, humiliation and death, knowing your eternal destiny is in his hands. "Forgive me, I didn't know," you say. But as I reflected, isn't that true of all sin?

A seventeen year-old young man was sentenced from twenty-seven years to life in jail yesterday in Milwaukee for killing a pizza deliveryman. After sentence was passed, he turned to the still grieving family and said, "I am sorry, I didn't understand what I was doing." After judgment is leveled in court for child abuse, drunk driving, killing someone, whatever the circumstance, the person will often turn to those still grieving and say, "I'm sorry. If I had to live my life over again…" That is what sin is—going for short-term joy and ignoring the long-term consequences.

But focus on Caiaphas. I've always seen him as a sleazy hypocrite. Maybe since I have been a bishop I don't look on spiritual leaders that way anymore. I'll bet he prayed every day. I'll bet he followed the instructions of his faith as best he could. He was balancing out all sorts of issues, including trying to guarantee that the Romans would not destroy the beloved temple, as the Babylonians had done. I'll bet he believed in the depth of his heart that he was doing the will of God.

That is what becomes scary. When our sinful desire becomes masked as God's will, then evil puts on saintly garments.

My wife and I just returned from New Zeland and Australia. Just before we arrived in Australia, the Prime Minister entered parliament and proclaimed that he was sorry for what the Australians had done to the aboriginal people of Australia. They had lived in that land 30-50,000 years before the first European settler arrived, and within less than 100 years, their population was decimated into one quarter of what it had been; they were shoved off all the land where they lived. And the Christian people of Australia decided they needed to do something or the aboriginals would be lost. They couldn't help the adults anymore, they felt, but they could the children. They could teach them to read and write and function in a modern society. So they passed a law that enabled the government to seize the children of the aboriginals, take them from their homes, and place them in Christian families and Christian orphanages. From 1900 to 1964 that was the law. It had a devastating effect on the aboriginal people and their children. I'll bet if you were one of those Christian families, taking a scared, confused aboriginal child into your home, you thought you were serving Jesus.

My theology professor at seminary once described the impact of original sin as a pencil turned upside down. When you think you're writing, you are erasing; and when you want to erase, you scribble. So often, we in the church mask what we think is God's will as our own. So often we have done incredible harm (true of all religions), and we justify unholy things because we believe it to be God's will.

We will all one day stand before this crucified One, and we may be filled with horror because of things we have done. There are things we have done because we believed it was God's will, when in reality it was only our prejudice. We have discriminated against people on the basis of age, race, sex, religion, etc., because we believed it to be what God wants. In a final moment of spiritual understanding we will pray, "God forgive us, we did not know what we were doing." May the Father heed these words of His dying Son.

Black marker

I often hear a song floating up from the basement where my daughter and her friends hang out on Saturday afternoons. I thought the song was called "Forgiveness" because in the refrain the artist's strong voice knowingly, lovingly calls out "Forgiveness! Forgiveness!" That's really all I knew about the song and I wanted to find out more, so I searched YouTube.

When I searched for "Forgiveness" it didn't bring up what I was expecting. It brought up a video inspired by a student's last words written in her journal before her death. The student was Mary Karen Read, killed in the Virginia Tech massacre. That was three years and three weeks ago. The four minute video is called, "Forgiveness."

In the beginning, a young blond man stands wooden, clutching a series of cards with writing on each of them. The camera holds his bitter face in its frame. He holds up the first card, staring intently over the top of it. It reads, "You neglected me." He says nothing. The camera moves to an old man seated, detached, watching. The young man drops the card to the floor.

The young man, lower lip quivering, holds up a second card. It reads, "You rejected me." Although his body remains motionless, the old man's pupils incline toward the words and his eyebrows knit around them.

The young man lifts a third card. It says, "Then you despised me." Years of regret fill the old man's eyes. The power he once wielded over this young man, was mocking him to wield it now—to save himself from this humiliation.

To the side of the young man's shoulder is a reflection of the old man. Near tears, the young man drops the last card and holds up another. It reads, "You killed mom." At these words it becomes clear the old man is reflected in a glass that separates him from his son. His prison blue shirt reflects his now naked guilt. The son, touching the next card, seems to be wagering what might remain of his father's dignity; yet, he is resolute in going on.

The next card reads, "You took everything from me." The father cannot save himself. Every card pierces him. Exposed, his shoulders hang and shake with what hadn't gone right, and what was left. The stillness is thick and foreboding, extinguishing the air behind the glass. One card remains. It's blank. Unexpectedly, the son draws a black marker out of his pocket. The father waits, helpless. Through tears of knowing and pain, the son writes. He holds the final card toward the broken man on the other side of the glass. It reads, "Father, I forgive you."

Mary Karen Read's last journal entry scrolls in spurts across the screen saying, "When deep injury is done to us, we never recover until we forgive. Forgiveness does not change the past. But it does enlarge the future."

Preemptive

Father forgive. Jesus speaks his first word, not to us, but to God. For three years he has spoken to us, preached, taught, exhorted and instructed us. Now as we have hung him up to die, Jesus turns from us and speaks to the father instead. Father forgive.

Having been those who were once directly addressed, we are now rendered bystanders, over-hearers of a conversation deep in the heart of the Trinity. Now at the end, the once adoring crowds are gone, and no one is left to listen to Jesus but the Father. The words he speaks to the Father are words that only God can dare speak to God—words of forgiveness, where only God can forgive. Father forgive, for they don't know what they are doing.

I spent most of my life trying to figure out what I am doing. I took a course at the seminary called Christian Ethics. It taught the weighing of various ethical options through careful rational deliberation, to choose the right course of action and to pursue it. I got an A in that course, but flunked it for the rest of my life. I—we—most often don't know what we are doing. "Well we thought we were standing up for law and order, following good biblical principles," the members of the Sanhedrin might have said. "We were just soldiers obeying orders; the government was in charge," the soldiers may have said. "Everything was done with the best legal advice," Pilate could say. And Jesus said, "they do not know what they are doing."

Wasn't that what the tempter promised us, back in the garden. We eat the fruit of the tree of knowledge and our eyes will be open. We will have knowledge like the knowledge of God. And we took, and we ate, and our eyes were opened. And we found that we were naked and afraid. Our new knowledge only exposed our vulnerability. They don't know what they are doing.

Matthew 25 contains one of the most nasty parables Jesus ever told; the parable of the great judgment. On his left were the goats—those who had not done good to the least of these. They had not recognized the incognito Christ, among the poor, the imprisoned and the oppressed. On the right hand are the sheep, those who have reached out to the least of these and are rewarded. But here is the shock. In the parable, the sheep talk just like the goats. We expect the goats to be clueless, but the sheep are just as dense. "When, Lord, did we see you?" The blessed sheep know enough to visit the prisoner, but they don't see Jesus any more clearly than the unethical apathetic goats. They don't know what they are doing.

How profound of Jesus to unite ignorance and forgiveness. We like to say that forgiveness is fine, so long as the perpetrator first knows and admits that what he was doing was wrong. First sorrow and repentance—only then forgiveness. Yet here today on the cross is pre-emptive forgiveness. Jesus first word is forgiveness. There will be no new world, no order out of chaos, no life out of death, without forgiveness first. Forgiveness is the first step, the bridge toward us that only God can build. The first word into our darkness is Father forgive. That is what Jesus meant when he said, in John's gospel, that there is no other way to the Father except through him. God will never get us except through forgiveness, forgiveness of our stupidity and cruelty. If God is going to wait until we know the wrong that we have done, then God will wait forever. And we don't have forever. Until then, we will be defensive, to deceitful, in our guilt. What—me conspire to kill and crucify the Son of God? Why pick on me? I'm doing the best I can. And of course, a lot better than others I know.

Did you ever notice that almost no one whom Jesus met on the brighter days in Galilee ever asked him for forgiveness? They asked him for many other things—most often healing. But Jesus knew that without forgiveness being the first word, there would be no meeting of God and humanity. First the word of forgiveness, and then at long last, the courage to tell the truth about who I am, what I have done or not done. We speak our words of confession in worship, not in order to receive forgiveness, but because we have already received it. At the cross, no one asked Jesus for forgiveness, yet he offered it. Father forgive them, they do not know what they are doing.

I've counseled abuse victims in a marriage, who were consumed by rage at their ex-spouse, even to the point of being a detriment to their own health and well-being. They found they finally had to forgive in order to leave the ex-spouse behind and get on with their life. They forgive in order to separate themselves. Jesus forgives in order to bind himself to us. Catholic bishops have faced the rage of victims of abuse by clergy, when there is any mention of the word forgiveness. No first, a lawyer, then restitution, and only then, maybe, forgiveness. I wonder if this is in part what led Jesus to be crucified. First he offered forgiveness to Samaritans, and adulterers and other supposedly unworthy sinners, then the offer of forgiveness to his persecutors. Have you ever had anyone offer you forgiveness when you didn't think you did anything wrong? It's disturbing. Even insulting. The cross is the price for preemptive forgiveness.

Forgiveness is what it costs God to be with people like us. Here on the cross, God had two possibilities—abandon us or abandon Jesus. God chose to let the Son hang there as a helpless victim of our ignorant evil. Today, this Friday, as Jesus hangs from the cross, we ponder the enormity of our cruelty and stupidity. But this day also, as Jesus speaks his first word, we first of all ponder the enormity of his grace. Father forgive them, they do not know what they are doing.

The Second Word from the Cross

One of the criminals who were hanged there kept deriding him and saying, 'Are you not the Messiah? Save yourself and us!' But the other rebuked him, saying, 'Do you not fear God, since you are under the same sentence of condemnation? And we indeed have been condemned justly, for we are getting what we deserve for our deeds, but this man has done nothing wrong.' Then he said, 'Jesus, remember me when you come into your kingdom.' He replied, 'Truly I tell you, today you will be with me in Paradise.' Luke 23:39-42

Prayer

Blessed are you, O Lord our God, today have joined us to eternity, through the death and sacrifice of your Son, in whose name we pray. Amen.

Being with Jesus

She was near the end of her life, already a long life. Now in her late eighties, she was growing weaker as she gradually succumbed to congestive heart failure. I asked her, "What are you feeling now? Are you afraid? Regretful? What do you feel?" She answered, "No not afraid; my main comfort is that soon I will get to be with Jesus." That was her great comfort as she came to the end; she would be with Jesus.

Of course it was a great comfort to her, because in a sense, a deep sense, she was already with Jesus. She had lived every day of her life, for as long as she could remember, with Jesus. Jesus for her was not just a future hope, but a present reality. She did not have to wait for death to be with Jesus; she was in paradise with Jesus already.

Having spoken to the heavenly Father, "Father forgive them; they don't know what they're doing," Jesus now speaks to a criminal—a rabble rowser, perhaps an insurrectionist, maybe more accurately a terrorist. The criminal said to Jesus, "Jesus, remember me when you come into your kingdom." He must certainly have been thinking about tomorrow. For today on a cross in horrible agony, and mocked before all the world, any kingdom promised by Jesus must be in some distant future time. But Jesus surprised him; "Today you will be with me in paradise."

Today. One might say that both were headed to death, on their way through death, therefore there they were on their way to paradise that comes after death. But I don't think that gets at the shock of what Jesus is saying here, and what he has been saying all along to his disciples. When Jesus talks about paradise, when he talks about the kingdom of God, he is not talking about a place where we go someday, rather he is talking about a relationship that we enter into today. How astounding then that Jesus would be talking about a paradise connected with the horror of his cross.

Paradise is wherever or whenever we are with Jesus. Our practice of the Christian faith is not our preparation for paradise; it is our participation in paradise. The eternal complete relationship with Jesus begins here, even if not now in its fullness. So we could say that paradise began for the criminal on the cross, when he recognized that the One who hung next to him in agony was his Lord, and the master of his life. Or maybe the thief didn't know any of that; as Jesus said, "they don't know what they're doing." All he said was, "remember me when you come into your kingdom," and that was enough.

Only God has eternal life. Nothing in us or in our world is eternal. Among us all that lives dies. Therefore if we are to have eternal life, we must somehow participate in God's life; be subsumed into God's existence, into God's story. Only God can do that, and whenever God does that, then that is eternal life—here now, then in all of its fullness.

This brief dialogue with Jesus and the criminal on the cross holds out the promise that, even in the worst situations of life, it is possible to be with Jesus. Our God is not a God who stands exalted on high, apart from the needs and troubles of this world. Rather, he is a God who gets mixed up in the mess of life. Even to the point of going with us criminals to the cross. In life, things can go from bad to worse, from worse to awful, and then there next to us is God, hanging there on the cross along with us.

The great Russian writer Leo Tolstoy compared his own conversion to that of the thief on the cross. "I, like the thief on the cross," he wrote, "have believed Christ's teaching and have been saved. This is no far-fetched comparison, but the closest expression of the condition of spiritual despair and horror at the problem of life and death, in which I lived formerly, and of the condition of peace and happiness in which I am now. I, like the thief, knew that I was unhappy and suffering. And suddenly I heard the words of Christ and understood them. Life-and-death ceased to seem to be evil; and instead of despair, I experienced happiness and the joy of life undisturbed by death."

Two thieves hanging on the cross and Jesus is there. Did he not say where two or three are gathered together there I am? Theologian Karl Barth called this the very first church. The church, indeed like paradise is wherever and whenever Jesus is with two or three of us. We righteous church people didn't get it when we criticized him for eating and drinking with sinners; we didn't get it when he said I've come to seek and to save the lost. It never occurred to us that the worst of sinners are those who do not know their sin; the worst of the lost are who do not know how lost we really are. Now the one who ate and drank with sinners dies with sinners; the word made flesh is born among us, heals and teaches, preaches and works miracles, is betrayed, suffers and dies. He walks into the halls of paradise with one miserable repentant thief as the prize for all of his work. And this he calls paradise.

To tell the truth Lord Jesus, we weren't that close to your cross when the soldiers nailed you to the wood and hoisted you up over Golgotha. But standing at a safe distance, we glory at your promise to the criminal. We have come to know our sin and lost-ness and we yearn for the paradise you promise. Give us faith in your words that today we may be in paradise with you, now, in part, and then in all fullness.

Through Baptism

Biblically speaking, we don't know much about the Paradise of which Jesus speaks in this second word from the cross. It points to the Garden of Eden, humanity's birth home, where we basked among all that we ever needed. Or maybe it is not as much of a place as a situation where what was expected, death, is exchanged for the unfathomable, everlasting life. Our collective images of paradise revolve around what it is not. Paradise is not work as usual. Paradise is not the long slog of the changing seasons where enveloping warmth gives way to bitter cold; sunshine, then days of heavy clouds. Our concept of paradise is a place of escape where we leave behind for a short time the mundane. Paradise is where little is expected of us, where the weather is pleasing to us, where flowers bloom year-round and small creatures need not hibernate. But even in our paradise, the reminder of death is as nearby as the closest beach.

My family was on a beach vacation on Ash Wednesday this year. We considered visiting a church but found no services early enough for our central time zone children. That first day of Lent, on the beach, I noticed a woman picking seashells with a smudge mark on her forehead. It took me a second glance to remember that is what Christians do on Ash Wednesday. We remember that we are here for a time, brought into the world from very little and returning to the earth one day.

As I crunched along the sea shell beach that day, I observed the simple fact that our spot of paradise formed over years and years of sea life that had died. After the death of a sea creature the tides push and pull tons of water over each shell left behind so that it slowly crushes those around it even as it crushes itself. Their red stripes, pink interiors, and purple dots become commingled into a blinding expanse of speckled white. Our children moved the sand into huge mounds and deep valleys with roads interconnecting each other. They dug into the sand with hands, feet and shovels, feeling the hot shells on the top that give way to cool, damp sand underneath. We walked on and played on and our youngest even tasted the beach that made our temporary earthly paradise. A paradise created by time and death.

Jesus speaks of Paradise from the cross where he is giving himself willingly. Here while he is slowly suffocating to death, he tells the stranger at his side that all of it—the deriding, the clothes, the crown of thorns, the criminal's confession, all of it—is at the threshold of a new paradise. This death leads to paradise. But it is not a Paradise from which we return, it is not for a time, it is for all time. Nor is it a paradise we finally visit when we die. Jesus, through his death on the cross, ushers into the world a new kingdom—a new creation—that frees us to live among each other without fear of each other. Jesus in ridding the world of its bondage to sin completes the creative work that he began when the world was nothing but a formless void.

On the first day, when there was the separation of waters, Jesus was taunted on the cross; when the sea creatures crawled into their shells and teemed in the ocean, the Messiah spoke tenderly to the criminal dying next to him. As the psalmist prayed, "I am poured out like water, and all my bones are out of joint; my heart is like wax…you lay me in the dust of death," already we hear these same words on Jesus' lips. When the angel stood before the shepherds and told them that today a Savior is born to you, even as Jesus cried out that first newborn night, already we hear him telling of new family arrangements.

God has birthed from this torturous death a family that knows first not what they believe, nor the nation in which they live, nor the denomination to which they belong, but a family that knows first that they are born through baptism into the great tribe of God's people.

Through this death we no longer have to pretend we are separated from each other. It is paradise right here, right now, even sitting in the midst of death this afternoon, that we can live and love one another as God has loved us. We can confess and forgive; we can worship God and serve the stranger. Jesus brings us into a paradise that is not for a time, not even a long time, but he brings us into God's time. God welcomes us into the kingdom that does not keep track of time in minutes and days but welcomes us any time, any day, to turn away from our fears, our sin, our separation and follow this way, the way of the cross.

Eden restored

"I say to you today you will be with me in paradise." Someone has said that we major in the minors. That is, we focus on the texture of the Eucharistic bread, instead of Christ himself. So also in hearing this second "word from the cross" we may focus on the "when," instead of the "whom." Instead of the promise that we will be with Christ in paradise, we worry the adverbial modifier: whether or not the thief will be with Jesus in paradise by midnight on Friday (as the "today you will be with me" might seem to suggest) or on whether "today" modifies the speaking verb ("Today I say to you"). We major in the minors.

Fortunately, in its more original form, the Greek text lacks any and all punctuation: the adverb may reasonably be thought to modify either the speaking or the being. Perhaps it modifies both. Either way, however, our focus on adverbial modification of either time or speech misses the point.

After all, in his plea the thief doesn't insist on being with Jesus today. In fact, he already is with Jesus; and, in point of faith, if paradise consists of being with Jesus, then even when crucified with Jesus, he is in paradise, though whether crucifixion with Jesus is the same as being with Jesus in his kingdom may seem doubtful. The thief had said, "Jesus, remember me when you come into your kingdom." And Jesus had replied, "I say to you today you will be with me in paradise."

Within the context of public execution, the mere mention of "paradise" may seem odd. The pathetic deaths of three human beings by crucifixion could hardly be further from almost any definition of "paradise." Though if, as may be the case, paradise (as in the Greek text of Genesis 2.8) refers to Eden, that first garden of primeval memory, this will not be the first death to occur in paradise. It was after all in Eden—in Paradise—that our first parents, disobeyed their creator and believed a lie that they too could be like God—and death enters Eden as our first parents are cast out. This, then, is not the first occasion in which evil will manifest itself in Paradise—if, indeed, the events of Golgotha occur in Paradise. But whether paradise or no, this will be the first occasion in which evil will fall prey to its own devices, such that death is put to death by means of the unjust death of the only innocent person ever born under law.

So it's not so much that Jesus died in Paradise, but that Jesus' death on Golgotha, his dying with a thief on either side, righteous Jesus dying as the epitome of unrighteousness, restores paradise—that is, it restores the creation to the Creator, restores us to God, and thereby makes all things new: Eden restored.

"Jesus, remember me when you come into your kingdom." In Eden, the fruit of the Tree of Knowledge yielded death. Now, on Golgotha, the Fruit of the Tree of the cross yields the kingdom of God, the rule of Christ, and the reign of life forever more. Here, Paradise is restored and a garden of death becomes the garden of life.

To be with Jesus is to be in paradise—whether now or then; whether today, tomorrow, or whenever. Being with Jesus, even in his death, is paradise. Being with Jesus at any time, in any place, is being in paradise. Baptized into Christ, we are in Eden; baptized into his death, we are with him in his kingdom. Joined to Christ's crucified body, we are eternally re-membered in his kingdom—all by means of the Lamb of God's death yesterday, today, and forever.

The Third Word from the Cross

When the soldiers had crucified Jesus, they took his clothes and divided them into four parts, one for each soldier. They also took his tunic; now the tunic was seamless, woven in one piece from the top. So they said to one another, "Let us not tear it, but cast lots for it to see who will get it." This was to fulfill what the scripture says, 'They divided my clothes among themselves, and for my clothing they cast lots.' And that is what the soldiers did.

Meanwhile, standing near the cross of Jesus were his mother, and his mother's sister, Mary the wife of Clopas, and Mary Magdalene. When Jesus saw his mother and the disciple whom he loved standing beside her, he said to his mother, 'Woman, here is your son.' Then he said to the disciple, 'Here is your mother.' And from that hour the disciple took her into his own home. John 19:23-27

Prayer

Pour your grace into our hearts, O God, that we who have known the incarnation of your Son, Jesus Christ, announced by an angel, may by his cross and passion be brought to the glory of his resurrection, for he lives and reigns with you in the unity of the Holy Spirit, one God, now and forever. Amen.

God-bearer

As I was thinking about this text, I could not get an idea out of my head. What was Mary thinking as she stood beneath the cross? I am not a mother, but I am a parent. I cannot imagine the agony she felt. It was not supposed to be like this. I wondered if she began to reflect on the visitation of the angel. Hail favored one, the Lord is with you. You will bear messiah; the One longed for will be your child. Maybe she remembered that giddy moment when visiting Elizabeth, whose yet unborn son leapt for joy in her presence. A handmaid of the Lord, she was.

But then things began to happen in ways that she could not imagine. Late in pregnancy she must travel a long route to Bethlehem. When she gets there, she gives birth not in a castle, not even with family surrounding her at home, but in a crowded stinky filthy stable filled with animals that brought the people to the inn—crowding her out. Yes, some shepherds came. Yes, some wise men came—but they were pagans. At the temple presentation an aged prophet named Simeon grasps the child and gives thanks that he was able to see the messiah before he dies, but then he turns to Mary and says, "a sword will pierce your soul." Even at age twelve they lose him, and struggle to find him in Jerusalem until they discover that he is questioning and challenging the religious leaders.

After Joseph is dead, this first-born son leaves and begins to preach. The word on the street is that he has lost his mind. The religious leaders think he is demonic. So she takes her other sons and rushes to Capernaum to talk to him—the word here in Greek means "to seize him." She is coming to bring him home. But when they arrive, there is no room to get close to him. When told that his family is there, Jesus says, "who is my family but those who do God's will." Was she thinking of all of this while she stood underneath that cross, watching her first-born, her child of promise, suffering and dying? It wasn't supposed to be like this.

Then Jesus sees her and says, "woman [in Greek a gentle term, not one of rebuke] look at your son." Look at your son. This is what the angel meant. This is what Messiah is to do. He is the Lamb of God who takes away the sin of the world, who suffers, who dies. This is what it is about. Then he says to John, standing next to Mary, "Behold your mother." And we are told she begins to live with him from that very hour. You see, it was the first-born son's task to care for the mother if the father died, and if he was about to die, to entrust her to someone else. Jesus does not entrust her to one of his younger brothers, but instead entrusts her to the Church; to John. And that was a gracious thing. That means she will be present on Easter Sunday. That means she will be present at Pentecost. Tradition tells us that John tended to her until she died at his home in Ephesus. Her faith affirmed.

The Orthodox Christians have a title for Mary: *Theotokos*. God-bearer. And so she is, for she bore the en-fleshed Word of God. She is our mother, as a church. We are, in some strange way, like her. We are anointed in Baptism, sealed with the Holy Spirit and marked with the cross of Christ forever, that we might go out and proclaim God's grace to all. We come to the table and take into ourselves the real presence of Jesus Christ in bread and wine. We bring him out into our world. We are the *Theotokoi*, if you will. God-bearers to a world not always ready to hear what we have to say. We often have pierced souls. The rich want to get richer, the powerful want more power, and far too often religious leaders see their task as using what they understand of God to condemn others and thereby lift up themselves. And our souls are pierced. Ah. But our faith will be vindicated. We may feel the pain of Friday, but Sunday will come.

Your heart's home

"Woman, your son," Jesus says. "Son, your mother." It is such a nice domestic scene. How thoughtful he is; how kind. Such a son for a mother to be proud. Here is one last gesture of filial concern. And it seems like a happy ending! "From that hour," the Evangelist says, "the disciple took her into his own home." Good old Mom, provided for with three squares a day, a place by the fire; social security benefits and all. Good old disciple, you could always count on him in a pinch. It's a touching scene; enough to bring tears to your eyes.

Except it's wrong: this isn't Jesus, dying some quiet Hollywood death in his own bed, surrounded by an adoring family, tidying up some last minute domestic business. Rather, this is a public execution, a sanctioned lynching. This is *mors turpsissima crucis*, the "most terrible death of the cross." The Romans themselves called it that, and reserved it for slaves and rebels and traitors. The faces around the cross are mostly not friends and family, but hired thugs, soldiers and a laughing, jeering mob. And the one dying is the Christ of God, the anointed one. But anointed now with his own blood, a crown of thorns digging into his scalp, spikes through his wrists and ankles, writhing in agony, croaking out his life. These are the arrangements. This is the victim.

And there's something more going on here than a nice, domestic arrangement. The "something more" is this: In this scene on Calvary, this precise scene, the human dimension of God's awesome work of salvation is laid out before us. It is here where we discover what the cross means for our life. Here we glimpse what Jesus' death means for how we live! Jesus went to the cross that we might be reunited with God—that's true, and that's what we proclaim today. But he also went to the cross that we might be reunited with one another! That's the human dimension. And that's what this scene is about.

I have a bone to pick with this translation: He said to his mother, "Woman, here is your son." Then he said to the disciple, "Here is your mother." It's just plain flatfooted; it lacks power, drama, and punch. And doesn't say what the Greek says. The older English translations had it better. King James, for instance, has it, "he saith unto his mother, Woman, behold thy son! Then saith he to the disciple, Behold thy mother!" It's the "behold" I miss. In Greek, the word is *idou*, and it sounds like a verbal trumpet blast…*idou! Idou!* What it says is this: Behold! Behold! Pay attention now! This important! I know…"behold" an old-fashioned word, and we want our translations up to date, but "Look" just doesn't do it, or "See" or worse, "here is." What happens when you gaze upon the face of your beloved, or your new-born child for the first time? Or what happens when you gaze upon the Grand Canyon, or Chartres Cathedral? You don't just take a look, or check it out, or even see, rather you behold! And it changes you!

Technically, *idou*, that verbal trumpet blast, is a "particle sentence," a word that stands for a whole command…and one size fits all: *Idou!* Behold! Whoever is here, whoever is in eyesight, Behold! Something big is happening! Don't miss it! We hear this blast almost 200 times in the New Testament: Behold! But here at the cross something interesting happens. The *idou* becomes *ide!* It becomes personalized, an imperative, second person singular: You behold! Mother, you behold you son! Disciple, you behold your mother! And it changes them: from that day he took her into his home!

This is what the cross does to us on a human level; it teaches, and it commends. The cross commands us, to behold one another. To behold in one another a mother, son, sister, father, daughter, and brother. "Look around you," this scene on the cross reminds us, "Look around you! Behold!" What do you see? Who do you see? An acquaintance? A friend? A relative? But mostly, we see strangers; unknown faces with unknown stories, with unknown needs and unknown pains and unknown dreams…and unknown perils and demands. And we pass through our life, our days as strangers ourselves, our names not known, our stories, needs, pains, all hidden! We wear our masks and disguises, our hoodies and our hats; and we pass unknown. What is worse, we pay a terrible price for the failure to see, to behold.

And so, we pass our days in loneliness and anger, in hatred and prejudice, in injustice and war. "But let me introduce you," says our Lord from the cross. "Let me introduce you to each other anew!" Because of God's mighty deed of reconciliation in Christ, you are no longer strangers—but friends—and closer than friends: the very family of God, united by God's love and mercy.

The invitation from the cross is this: To behold and take one another into your heart's home! Be with one another as a people at home with the family. Provide for the wants. Heal the hurts! Right the wrongs! Look beyond the narrow vision that sees only a few known and familiar faces and behold this new family that God creates from the cross! This is what the cross-shaped love of God is about: making home for us in the heart of God. This is what the cross is about in this world: making home for one another! And this reconciliation with God is the starting place for our reconciliation with each other, "Woman, behold your son! Son, behold your mother! Behold!"

A mother's love

Jesus' Third Word from the cross is a word about the human community of which all of us are part. It may not have the powerful impact of the word before, nor does it have the searching cry of the word that follows. But here is a word of Jesus that has a quality all of its own, a quality of human compassion and caring love: "Woman, here is your son." . . ."Here is your mother."

We can imagine, of course, that it was a mother's love that brought Mary to the cross that Friday afternoon. Where else would she be? As hard as it was and as much as it must have pained her, Mary was there for the same reason any mother or father would have been there—she loved her son. In a way, his cross was her cross. The poet Kipling captured it in the words:

> "If I were hanged from the highest hill,
> Mother o'mine, O mother o'mine!
> I know whose love would follow me still,
> Mother o'mine, O mother o'mine!'

Fortunately, Mary was not alone. Her sister was there; so was Mary Magdalene and Mary the wife of Clopas. And so was a man often called the "beloved disciple." the disciple who, according to Scripture, "Jesus loved." Jesus had brothers, but where were they? Jesus had other disciples, but where were they? Were they so ashamed or so afraid that they hit the road? Scripture doesn't say.

But now, Jesus takes notice of them—his mother and the "beloved disciple." And when he does, he speaks. "Woman", he says—an address of deep respect in the language of the day— "Woman, here is your son." And then, motioning again with his head and his eyes, he says to the disciple: "Here is your mother." And, says the Scripture, "the disciple took her to his own home."

Even there, in the darkness of the hour, in the agony and the mockery, Jesus' concern is for his loved ones. He shows us that those relationships that are part of human community are relationships that matter. He shows us that we are called to care for one another. He shows us a vision for the church that is crucial for our witness.

The Third Word of Jesus from the cross is a powerful reminder that while we are part of a family of mother and father, sisters and brothers, or whatever, we are also part of a much larger family, a global family, a family so desperately in need of love these days. All of us belong to one another. That's the way God created us and Christ died to keep us that way.

The elderly woman in the nursing home—she is your mother. The young man who is struggling with acceptance of his homosexuality—he is your son or your brother. The young woman who is trying to put her life back together after an abusive marriage—she is your daughter or your sister. The man who cries because he can find no work to provide for his wife and children—he is your father or your brother.

The Third Word from the cross is a word about the human community of which all of us are part. It is worth considering that in this Word from the Cross Jesus is setting in motion something he said another time: "Just as you did it for one of these, you did it for me!" Just because we have it heard so many times before, doesn't make it any less true. In his dying breath Baron von Hugel said: "Caring is the greatest thing, caring matters most." He seemed to understand that death is not the greatest tragedy. The greatest tragedy is to have lived without caring for others.

As we gather with Mary and the beloved disciple at the foot of the cross, we can hear Jesus say: "Mother, here are your sons and daughters; sisters and brothers, here is your mother!'

The Forth Word from the Cross

From noon on, darkness came over the whole land until three in the afternoon. And about three o'clock Jesus cried with a loud voice, *'Eli, Eli, lema sabachthani?'* that is, 'My God, my God, why have you forsaken me?' When some of the bystanders heard it, they said, 'This man is calling for Elijah.' At once one of them ran and got a sponge, filled it with sour wine, put it on a stick, and gave it to him to drink. But the others said, 'Wait, let us see whether Elijah will come to save him.' Matthew 27:45-29

Prayer

O Christ, we have come again today to try to understand the mystery of your crucifixion. We don't understand why you couldn't save us without the suffering and the blood and the despair, but while we don't fully understand, we laud you and honor you. We are immensely grateful for you today and we know you love us. Amen.

Not the God we want

Darkness surrounded Jesus when he said these words. But then Jesus did some of his best work in the dark. He walked on water and stilled the raging sea just before dawn. He taught Nicodemus at night. He celebrated his most famous meal on a Thursday evening. And rose from the dead while it was still dark. Easter happened when it was dark.

But this was the darkest darkness for our Lord, and what words, what terrible frightening words this middle dark word from the cross: "My God, my God, why have you forsaken me?" These words, of course, were not original with Jesus. They are a quote from Psalm 22 and they are words that Jesus learned by heart, probably when he was just a child. Jesus is doing what we often do when we are at the end of our rope. There, sophisticated thoughts wither and we're forced to reach down into the recesses of our memory to something we learned in childhood. The Lord's Prayer perhaps, or the 23rd Psalm.

For Jesus, during that dark afternoon of suffering, it was "My God, my God, why have you forsaken me?" "Why are you so far from helping me?" This from the one who was so intimate with God the Father that he once said, "I and the Father are one." And "If you have seen me, you have seen the Father." Now though there is a profound separation, a distance, as he says, "Where are you God?" "Where ARE you God?" We've asked that before, haven't we? We asked it when religious zealots flew airplanes into the towers in New York, when the tsunami killed 230,000 in Indonesia, when the 9.0 earthquake hit Japan just this year. Or, when our marriage failed. Or, when the medical tests came back positive. Or, even when our candidate lost the election and the government was going to hell. "Where were you my God and why are you so far from helping me?" And there was no answer, was there?

God did not rush in to save us from natural or manmade disaster or from the disasters we make of our own lives. Do you ever get so disappointed in God that you are actually angry with him? Do you ever get so angry with God that you stop talking to him? Stop going to church? Sure you have. As have I. Most of my prayers, you see, are God give me this, God grant me that, God deliver me, rescue me, save me, and the ones I love. And what we should be praying is God preserve me from trying to get you to run the world on my own terms. Save me from trying to get my life to work out the way that I want. Help me to understand when my Lord asks from the cross "Why have you abandoned me, God?"

Let's accept it: God is not the kind of god that we wanted. He's not a god who works the world always to our benefit. He doesn't swoop down mightily to fix everything that goes wrong in life. He's not a god who is just like us, only stronger. He's not a god who when things get dark, immediately switches on the lights. Rather, He comes to hang out with us, in the dark, on a cross, and lets us in on the most intimate of conversations within the very heart of the Trinity.

"God, why have you abandoned me?" There is a mystery here beyond our knowing and a pathos beyond our understanding. The Son of God has come to us and loved us to the point of taking our disasters, our failures, upon himself. Living a righteous life, he has become the bearer of our tragic sinfulness; a sinfulness that separates him from a loving and righteous God the Father.

The Trinity, which is inherently indivisible, is divided by love, by suffering, and ultimately by death. The sacrifice is massive and the Son calls out across the divide to the Father in words first inspired by the Holy Spirit, "My God, my God, why have you forsaken me?" And that is why I offer you these words today as words of hope. If you have been disappointed in God the fixer, then come today to know God the lover, God the sufferer, God the sacrifice. Where is God when darkness comes into our lives or into our world? He's there in the darkness with us, not preserved from life's horrors, but present in the midst of them. Though he was in the form of God, he did not regard equality with God is something to be exploited, emptied himself; and being found in human form, he humbled himself and became obedient to the point of death; even death on the cross.

God has a more complex notion of power and victory than we have. The Lord does not use our weapons, or our solutions. He does not share our sentimental definition of love. Nor does he despise or reject words of deepest anguish and doubt. It must indeed be a great God who can be prayed to with words as tough as Jesus words today. And someone must have deep, great faith to be able to pray this honestly to God: "My God, my God, why have you forsaken me?"

Journey by night

The back screen door slammed as Peter walked into their kitchen. Returning from an afternoon of playing with a friend down the street, the four year old yelled out, "I'm home. Got anything to eat?" Peter's mom appeared at the kitchen doorway and busied herself with some cookies and milk, while asking, "How was your afternoon with Billy?" "Oh, we had a great time" was the reply. "What did you?" his mom asked. "Oh, I helped Billy fix his bike," Peter joyfully responded. "Oh really," she replied. "I didn't know you knew how to fix a bicycle." "Oh, yeah it's easy," the son said. "When I got there Billy was sitting in his driveway crying. So, I asked him what was wrong. He said his bike was broken." "So, what did you do?" his mom asked. Peter replied, "I just sat down and cried with him. We cried for a while, then I gave him a hug and then we played on the swing-set. It was a great afternoon."

Here we have a simple story. A common childhood story that occurs daily in backyards. Or perhaps it is a story that parallels some of the events of holy week. A simple lesson, yet a profound one. It gives us an insight into the forsakenness of Christ on the cross. In his innocent ways, Peter claims he fixed the bicycle of his friend without even turning a wrench or pumping a flat tire. In a child-fresh wisdom, he knew that the problem was not that the bicycle would not work, but the problem was his friend was alone—disappointed and frustrated. The cure was not a repaired flat tire, but the presence of the friend. The fix was successful, because now the friend had someone with whom he could cry.

I serve as chaplain at a large nursing home and retirement center—the Skaalen Home in Stoughton, Wisconsin. In serving there almost nineteen years, I have learned at least one lesson about ministry. In the midst of almost overwhelming loss, or pain, or confusion, or fear, most people are not seeking an answer to their crisis. Rather they desperately need to know that they are not alone; they need someone to join them in their darkness. Late nights in the emergency room, or long days at the bedside of a dying person and their gathered family, or anguished encounters at the crisis intervention center at the hospital, these are all times of darkness. All are times when we need someone to enter our dark place with us.

Isn't this what Christ is doing for us and with us on the cross? By entering into the darkness, the isolation, the aloneness, the forsakenness, Christ goes into our darkness even before we get there. We reflect today on that event. In our fourth word from the cross, where Christ cries out in his forsakenness, we find irony. Christ so completely alone on the cross, in the resurrection becomes completely present. Christ was forsaken so that we don't have to be alone. God went into the darkness, so our darkness would not be so dark. God is present in the darkness, walking with us. Alfred Noyce in his poem entitled Night Journey put it this way:

Alone

No doubt that you have an image of what it must have been like for Jesus on Good Friday, on the cross. Maybe your picture of the crucifixion is from some piece of artwork, or a film. Maybe you have had the misfortune of seeing a passion play. One might even hope your image comes from having heard the stories year after year in church on this day. Wherever your image comes, many of you know by heart the seven words, the last words, from the cross. All these words, these last words, so in keeping with Jesus, his mission, his authority, his faith and love. From that very first sovereign pronouncement of divine mercy, to the last peaceful exhalation into death, Jesus uses the cross as a pulpit; one last proclamation of God's grace, hanging on a cross.

"My God, my God, why have you forsaken me," Jesus says. It is different from the other words, you know, unique in a couple of ways. For one thing, only Matthew and Mark report it, not Luke or John. And it's the only word these two gospels report. It may be that for a almost full generation of the early church, Matthew and Mark were the only written gospels. If so, then it is quite possible some of those first Christians only heard this word from the cross. If Luke and John had not come along to report other six words—theirs is a kind of wordy Jesus—we'd all be out of here by now. Finally, it's the only word we hear in Jesus' own language, in Aramaic: *"Eli Eli, lama sabachthani."* In this word, we are given the impression of being ear-witnesses to Jesus' own bitter cry on dying day.

Also different is this: this is an embarrassing word. The other words from the cross are a comfort. In some sense, they are in keeping with our image of Jesus in charge, even on the cross: forgive them, behold your mother, today in paradise, into your hands. But this word shrieks of pain, abandonment, anxiety and fear. We do not know what to make of it. We have tried to explain it, to make it more palatable, more comfortable. Jesus is quoting Psalm 22, a Psalm of lament. Like other psalms of lament, it begins in desolation, but it ends with a proclamation that God will help: "But you, O Lord, be not far away!" So this desolate word is not really so desolate at all, but an assertion of faith, of hope, by the dying Jesus.

Why these words? Of all the words of the Psalms, why these haunted words? Wouldn't it be simpler to acknowledge that Jesus, here as elsewhere in his ministry, speaks plainly? That he utters on the cross in his anguish his own sense, his feeling and pain at the absence of God in the awful hour? It's as if we were trying to protect Jesus from the experience, the awful experience of god-forsakenness! To make these words seem more palatable is to try to say that Jesus never really knew what it felt like to be alone, abandoned, or desolate. If that's the case, he never really knew what it is like to be human.

It is this word from the cross that seems like it is my word, and God knows, it has been often enough. Who of us has not experienced what it is like to be godforsaken! Have we never felt abandoned by the world, left out, and left behind, by friends, by family, by God. Sometimes in small ways the sense of desolation creeps up on us as unresolved guilt, a sorrow that won't go away, or that persistent question of whether there is any meaning to it all. We have experienced life dragging along, belly in the dust, from one damn dull day to another, with no apparent point. We have each of us experienced anxiety, emptiness and uncertainty. To be human is to feel this way at times, vulnerable, isolated, and alone. It is part of our daily fare, our daily condition.

And sometimes, bad times, it sweeps over us in great waves. And our question is: who can comfort in the face of such sorrow? Who can forgive such guilt? Who can soothe such pain? And the word becomes my word and your word: 'My God, my God, why?'

And here is Jesus on the cross, and the word of the prophet hangs over the whole scene: He has borne our grief, and carried our sorrows. He has known the full range of our needs, drained the full cup of our sin to the dregs. And then this word makes it clear. This is the heart of the cross: the Christ, the anointed One of God, has taken upon himself our very god-forsakenness, yours and mine, and delivered into the heart of God. This is what the cross proclaims: that though we may feel very much alone, sometimes, at times often; but we are not alone, for God is with us. In Christ, God has been with us, is with us, will be with us...even in the god-forsaken times of life; though that answer may not come easily or immediately. That cry was not the last word. Easter dawns with a shout of victory, God's own shout out of the tomb. And with it, all the god-forsakenness is cast away, and the darkness is shattered by the rising light of God's love.

The Fifth Word from the Cross

After this, when Jesus knew that all was now finished, he said (in order to fulfill the scripture), 'I am thirsty.' A jar full of sour wine was standing there. So they put a sponge full of the wine on a branch of hyssop and held it to his mouth. John 19:28-29

Prayer

O thou Thirst divine, O longing Heart, O dry and thirsting Lamb of God, be thou the water of life for us; quench our thirsting souls; flood us in your dying, that we might live, in the Name of the Father, and of the Son, and of the Holy Spirit. Amen.

Melody and meaning

Could it be that the whole life of Jesus was and is nothing but the fulfillment of scripture? What would it mean if Jesus' every act and deed were nothing more than the completion of some biblical word or phrase? On the one hand, I suppose, it might sound rather robotic and boring. But, on the other hand, would it be so bad to live a life in complete obedience to the Word of God? Yet, again, what else could the Word of God do? He who is himself the very message of the scriptures, the melody and meaning of the sacred page, could he do or be anything but the fulfillment of that written word? Even as the Apostle says when writing to the Corinthians, "Christ is the Yes to all God's promises."

It is, therefore, no surprise that Christ speaks and acts to fulfill scripture. The surprise is that he so speaks and so acts for us and for our benefit. The surprise is that he so speaks and acts not only for those who take time on Good Friday (or any earthly day for that matter) to sit and listen and sing and pray and contemplate the depths of his passion. But he does so for all who, this day and every day, trundle along University Avenue oblivious to his cries, earphones in place, listening to the news or to the latest band or to a podcast of Bon Appetite on how to baste your favorite barbeque. Perhaps, following these few hours, we too will be on our way to something more important: a class, the coffee shop, a job, a workout, a film, or to visit a friend and enjoy a drink at a local watering hole where happy hour will afford us enough liquid diversion to quench our banal thirst and attenuate the pain of this parched and pathetic Lamb of God.

Behold the Lamb of God trussed up and basted for a cosmic barbeque: spitted, he declaims before the fire, "I thirst." Like the Psalmist of old, the dying Lamb thirsts for God; he thirsts for water in a dry land; he thirsts for meaning amid a death overflowing with absurd humiliation, abuse, and vilification. His torturous death may momentarily satisfy our thirst for news of misery, murder, and mayhem. Perhaps, on his account, we will temporarily have had enough.

Perhaps tonight we will not need the same old "news" with its tales of murder, mayhem, and money. He suffers all the malevolence for which we thirst. His thirst quenches our thirst for the blood sport of Cain—that we might drink his paschal blood and never thirst again. This man dry as dust becomes for us, and for all the dying oblivious world, the spring of water welling up to eternal life.

Treading our path

I grew up outside of Chicago and each night my parents would watch the WGN 9:00 pm news. You could count on three things. First, there would be a weather forecast from a beloved meteorologist. Second, sports news about the Cubs, Sox, Bears, Bulls, and Blackhawks. And finally there would be a story that began with "Shots have been fired outside of Cabrini Green." Or, "Two were murdered last night in gang violence at Cabrini Green."

Cabrini Green was the home to 15,000 people living in 3,600 apartments. The intent was for mixed-income and affordable housing on the North side, the affluent side, of Chicago. The complex was named after Sister Frances Cabrini—the first American Saint; and in true Illinois fashion, this was the worst way to honor her ministry and life calling. Not long after completion in the 1960s, the apartments of Cabrini Green became home to the very poor, and it quickly became the model of how to trap people into deep and hopeless poverty.

The residents of the apartments were nearly all African American. This was the home to the fabled Welfare Queen of the 1980s. I now think that hearing the stories about Cabrini planted many seeds of racism in me that I struggle with to this day.

It was a world I didn't understand, nor did I want to. I couldn't begin to understand that the kids my age who lived there were just like me. Over years, the conditions grew so terrible that after several lawsuits, the City of Chicago began the process of tearing down the buildings. The last building was torn down a year ago, and today after decades of horrific stories, Cabrini is no longer making the news.

I spent last weekend in Chicago, and as much as I thought through the routes we would travel that day, I only thought about EL stops and streets. Not neighborhoods. Well into our march down Chicago

Avenue we came upon a large open lot. At first we saw a huge community garden—a welcome site for Madison visitors. But a few steps down the block was a massive open field with beautiful grass. It took me a few seconds, but it soon hit—this was Cabrini Green. The killing fields of Chicago were now quiet. Here it was—that verse from "Lift Every Voice and Sing" brought to life,

> "We have come over a way
> that with tears has been watered;
> we have come, treading our path
> through the blood of the slaughtered."

For the residents of the affluent neighborhoods nearby, the clearing of Cabrini Green was an empty tomb moment—the buildings had been rolled away and what was left was open space. It was no secret that Cabrini was a mistake and a complete disaster. But woven into that failed experiment were 15,000 lives. Everyone wanted the violent world of Cabrini to come to an end—especially those living in the apartments.

For those on the outside, tearing down the complex and building new and less cramped affordable housing somewhere else would be a real resurrection story. Except for the fact that only a fraction of the apartments being destroyed were replaced with new housing. As the building was being scheduled for demolition, the residents would soon lose their homes, but without any affordable places to move to. The residents, who had cried out time and time again for help, were now asking that the buildings not be torn down, not just yet.

Our passage is of Jesus suffering, of crying out for something. And yet what he received—vinegar, was worse than being thirsty. Jesus received a liquid, but a liquid that would remind him of his place, suffering as an accused criminal on a cross. Jesus was reminded again of the people who rejected him. And it was a bitter reminder that when you seek something you need, to be completely filled, and truly loved and respected, you won't find that here on earth from others.

As the buildings of Cabrini Green fell, it was tempting to think of this moment as a resurrection—an entire community died, and what was left was an empty grave. But, what looked like a resurrection to those on the outside was in fact not a resurrection for many. In fact it was a bitter end for these families. And it was a bitter reminder their suffering would continue as a people now in an impoverished Diaspora.

When Jesus' death finally came, it was the cross that was left behind. The cross stays here on earth, in every corner of pain, suffering and uncertainty. As long as we see the cross, we cannot be fooled into thinking that wiping out one "problem" is good for everyone. It's when we don't look for the cross that we think we are living in a just world, a world where all can bear life's pains alone. Sadly, it takes these moments when we cry out in our own pain, thirsting for compassion, that we taste the true brokenness of our world. But the cross was left behind for those times in life when we are given something so bitter we cannot bear it. Thank God, the cross was left behind.

Sour

Just two little words, "I thirst." It sounds like such a simple thing. To thirst is as basic a need as it gets. Our bodies need liquid, and Jesus is human, after all.

Many of the Lenten texts we have read over the last few weeks refer to our own thirst. We recall from Psalm 63, "Oh God, you are my God, I seek you, my soul thirsts for you, as in a dry and weary land where there is no water."

In an existence of plenty, we may not even recognize our own bodily thirst. Diet experts claim that we sometimes eat food when we are really thirsty and a drink of water will fill that need. How about our soul's thirst? Do we recognize it? Do we know what will fulfill that need? Or do we fill it with the trappings of this world? Whether we know it or not, we are thirsting for God—our creator and sustainer.

"I thirst." At first glance, it may seem like Jesus was trying to prolong his life. He had already endured a night of beating, the physical agony of this torturous death; the humiliation of hanging there, stripped of his clothing; a common criminal. In fact, hanging there among criminals. But John tells of the crucifixion in a very different way from the other Gospels. Jesus is handed over by Pilate and even carries his own cross. There are almost more words about the description of the scene and the discussion of the sign hanging above Jesus' head than description of the crucifixion itself.

Jesus has even made provision for his mother, giving her to the disciple that he loved. We can almost anticipate the end. The author even manipulates our minds and moves us in that direction by telling us that, "Jesus knew that all was finished." Oh, but wait! It is not quite finished. Jesus speaks again. Oh, and there is that phrase in parenthesis we may have skipped over. So why include this little detail? It says right there, "In order to fulfill scripture." In case we had any doubt that this is the Messiah of whom the prophets foretold, we get a little reminder. Jesus receiving the sour wine is not a gesture of mocking him, but a reference to the words in the Psalms, "he was given sour wine."

Not only of the words of the prophets in the Psalms but we get even more reminders of the life to which this man, this messiah, was called. We are reminded that Jesus' first miracle was turning water into wine at the wedding at Cana. He starts his ministry with the best wine and ends with sour wine. On a deeper level, Jesus' words recall his question to Peter at the arrest, "Am I not to drink the cup that the Father has given me?" Jesus' thirst thus symbolizes his willingness to embrace his death, and the offering of sour wine takes on an ironic note as just one more example of the world's misunderstanding of him. Here we see the thirst of the one who is himself the source of "living water." This is how we quench our own thirst, with the living water, with Jesus.

Jesus drinks the cup, the cup that was given to him by God. "I thirst." So they put a sponge full of the wine on a branch of hyssop and held it to his mouth.

Looking up

Given the weather outside, this may be difficult to believe, but a month ago—the first Sunday in March—I was walking on a frozen Lake Mendota with members of the youth group. As we looked up at the stars, we picked out the Big Dipper in the Northern sky; from there, Polaris, the North Star; and Orion in the South. Lee Powell pointed out Mars and the Pleiades. As I looked at the constellations, I started to ponder how far they were from each other—and from us.

The stars in Orion's belt are, on average 1,000 light years (or about 5.8 quadrillion miles) away. If one of its stars, Betelgeuse, was at the center of our solar system, it's surface would extend out to between the orbits of Mars and Jupiter. This made me think of the beautiful poem that opens the Gospel of John: "In the beginning was the Word, and the Word was with God, and the Word was God. He was in the beginning with God. All things came into being through him, and without him not one thing came into being. What has come into being in him was life, and the life was the light of all people. The light shines in the darkness, and the darkness did not overcome it."

Why am I reading a passage that we usually hear at Christmas? To once again ignite the flames of debate between science and religion? Certainly not—I am above all a Christian, but I also am a scientist by trade. I have heard that debate *ad nauseum*. I read the poem because that same Word, through whom all things were made, is now nailed to the cross. Because the light shines even on this darkest of days, because we must remember that the Word of God became flesh and we nailed that flesh to a cross.

As Luther warns, "You must get this through your head and not doubt that you [we] are the one who is torturing Christ, for your sins have surely wrought this." I also read the poem to remind us of the beginning as we approach the end. As the Gospel states "Jesus, knowing that all was now finished, and to fulfill the Scripture, said, 'I thirst.'"

I realize that the next meditation will center on the words, "It is finished," so I will focus on the words "I thirst." What was Jesus thirsty for? Maybe he really was thirsty. After all, he had been beaten, had carried his cross until he collapsed, and had been crucified for close to three hours. He had lost a lot of blood and water by that point.

Still, I believe that there is a deeper meaning. In the fourth chapter of John, Jesus tells the Samaritan woman, "Whoever drinks of the water that I shall give him will never thirst; the water that I will give him will become in him a spring of water welling up to eternal life."

It is doubtful, at this point, that Jesus thirsts for water. Instead, as the Biblical scholar Raymond Brown notes, Jesus asks his disciples in the Garden of Gethsemane, "Shall I not drink the cup which the Father has given me?" In the other three Gospels, Jesus prays that the cup might pass from him, but does submit to the will of the Father when he stipulates "not my will, but thy will".

The Gospel of John sees things a little differently: Jesus prays in the Garden saying, "Now my soul is troubled, and what shall I say? Father, save me from this hour? No, for this purpose I have come to this hour." In John's account, Jesus is determined to drink the cup that he is given to the last painful drop.

When the bystanders hear the cry of thirst, they take a branch of hyssop—the same material used to spread blood of the sacrificial lamb on the doorposts and lintel during the observance of Passover. On that hyssop, they offer a sponge soaked in vinegar. What mother, when her child is thirsty gives her child vinegar? It's just not something you do. It seems to be yet another insult.

Last evening at Maundy Thursday service, Pastor Pohlman reminded us that Jesus provided food and drink for and washed the feet of his betrayer. He forgives his disciples when they abandon him. Walking home last night, I looked up at the stars, and again was filled with awe.

But the beauty of the stars cannot compare to the beauty of what Jesus did for us this day. Yet, it is this same Savior and Lord, who, when we, through our sins, offer vinegar, says to us, "Come to the feast which I have prepared. Come, drink the water that I give you. Come, eat of my body, and drink of my blood."

The Sixth Word from the Cross

When Jesus had received the wine, he said, 'It is finished.' Then he bowed his head and gave up his spirit. John 19:30

Prayer

O Lord Jesus Christ, by your death you have taken away the sting of death. Grant unto us your servants so to follow in faith where you have first led the way, that at length we, too, may finish the work set before us, fall peacefully asleep in you, and at your call rise to live and serve you in all eternity—you who abide with the Father and the Holy Spirit, one God, now and forever. Amen.

Fruition

"It is finished," Jesus cries. Done. The end. Finito. Byeah, byeah, that's all folks. Nothing more to see here; may as well go. You can move on. You can go home now. Wait—before you pack up, we should ask this: What is finished? This service? Jesus' pain and suffering? His passion? His death? The cruelty received at the hands of the powerful? The suffering of the innocent One? It is now all ended. Jesus is finished; now delivered into the hands of a greater power (or at the least, into the cold grave).

Finished. Of course, if all he meant was that his life is finished, then it is merely a last biographical detail. This requires no faith; there were witnesses after all. There were soldiers and thugs, bureaucrats and bystanders. Then there was the fickle crowd that cheered on Sunday; jeered on Friday. Also, there were his once-upon-a-time disciples that would follow him to death, unless he actually went there, now mostly incognito. All were witnesses to that particular end.

Perhaps he meant his life is finished, his story. He breaths his last, John says. But he would be wrong then. We know this story is not finished. There is a sequel. The story goes on; there is a different conclusion. No one expected a surprise ending, worked by God. There is resurrection ahead, new life, a life beyond death.

His life finished? Why it's hardly begun. That would be harder to believe, yet we could. We do. For there have been witnesses! The women, faithful in their duties even to the end, are surprised at the tomb. Disciples, recalled from their hiding, are surprised on the road, or at the table. He is risen, they will say.

Perhaps he meant that his ministry is finished; his being among the people—healing, teaching, feeding. Perhaps this is what is all finished.

Yet that cannot be true either, for we know his ministry is among us still; still healing, teaching and feeding. We are witnesses.

So what is finished? To answer that we have to know what "finished" means. It does not merely mean brought to an ending; come to an end; this much and no more. There is a word in the New Testament, in Greek, for that sort of end—*eschatos*. It means, the last things, no more after this, but it's not the word used here. Here the word is *telos*, meaning to be brought to fulfillment, to completion, even brought to fruition. Finished in the sense of a goal attained.

Here on the cross his suffering, his life, his ministry all come to fruition. Here in the cross, the goal is reached. Mission accomplished—this time for real!

And that mission is nothing less than our salvation, our healing, our restoration, our reconstruction as the people of God! That is what is finished here: We are finished. Us. A saved people. And that word is the hardest one to believe!

We finished? Our healing finished? Our reconciliation finished? But isn't there something we need to do, must do?

Despite what Jesus says about it is finished, we always want to add a little bit more to the mission. To the mission, to the life of Jesus, to the cross, we want to add a bit more: the cross plus our strong belief, plus our good intentions, plus our sincerity, plus our regular worship, our prayer, our stewardship, our this and our that.

We always want to add something to what God did that Good Friday with Jesus on the cross. We say, or think, "Thank you, Lord, for your good efforts, and now we'll finish our part, and then won't you ever love me!" We are never quite willing to say with Jesus, "It is finished. Nothing more need to be done; God has done it all. Now nothing can be added. Not a thing."

We want to keep a hand on our redemption; that is the problem. That of course is sin, the old last enemy, here at the foot of the cross, making one last stab at destroying us. Of course it is bad news, this plus we would add to Jesus.

Because, if we are honest, we must say our best works arise from a mixed bag of good and bad motives. Our best faith always mingled with doubt; our best intentions and most sincere thoughts, muddled with self-deception and compromise. Every time we add our plus to Jesus, we run into the same old blank wall, and find ourselves mired in sin—in darkness and bondage still. As Pogo said, "We have met the enemy, and they is us."

The good news is there is no "plus" to Jesus. "It is finished," he cried, he announces, he proclaims from the Cross. Complete, fulfilled, done, nothing more is needed! *Satis est*, Luther said—it is sufficient. Anything else we may ever do...all our loving deeds, our faith, our sincerity, our worship, our praise, is just response to this all sufficient deed of God! In the cross, we are set free, from the enemy that is us, to live before God, confident, finally, that all that is needful has been done. It is finished. We are finished. And perhaps our first, our only response, to Jesus' word, "It is finished" is to bow our heads in wonder, and great astonishment, and say, "Thanks be to God!"

Resistance

Look up this passage in some commentaries and you may be surprised that the word that pops up in relationship to this text is "triumph." Of course, triumph is part of the discussions about texts in general for Good Friday. It's just that triumph doesn't seem right to me. For one thing, it's premature, like hearing Christmas music in Advent. It's too early to hear Easter trumpets.

Also triumph can be misunderstood to mean Jesus' suffering on the cross was divinely sanctioned, when the violence against Jesus came from this world. The whole scenario was unconscionable and put in motion after a consensus among misguided people. There was never any trial, but rather a lynching. I'm not left hearing trumpets, but reflecting on how this could happen?

I wonder how I am misguided. How is our society aligned with powers that do not always serve good, but rather unhealthy systems of power?

I think it's better to use the word "resistance" instead of triumph for Jesus on this day, because although Jesus was handed over to the authorities he did not hand over his authority. He did not acquiesce to the powers that led him to his death. He wasn't on the cross because he was successfully completing his task as someone meant to suffer. Rather his role was to bring in the reign of God, and the cross was the result.

Theologians such as Denny Weaver talk about nonviolent atonement and warn about how we may perceive triumph on the cross as meaning Jesus' suffering fulfilled the will of a God.

Many years ago during my internship one of the pastors, someone who was close to retirement, during a sermon talked about a woman going to his office and saying, "You know I try to practice what you preach about the cross and forgiveness, but the more I forgive my husband the more he hits me." She said she was trying to follow this path God has led her down but that it was difficult.

The pastor was pretty stunned. He hadn't considered how some of the things he said about the cross might be understood by someone stranded in oppression. And the experience altered him. As a young intern I was impressed that a pastor so old could be altered, but now that I am much closer to the age he was at that time, it doesn't surprise me as much that his experience changed the way he talked about the cross. I think it's good to be converted many times in our lives at all ages.

A child being bullied at school, a man tormented in a relationship, a woman berated at work might identify with Jesus on the cross and that may be healing for them. It is healing for all of us to know Christ identifies with our pain. But this message is not about Jesus being compliant with the violence inflicted upon him, leading us down a path of passively accepting injustice and believing our suffering is divinely willed and sanctioned by God. Rather Jesus was resistant.

The next year at seminary one of my professors, Lynn Osiek, said something that has stayed with me: "Jesus didn't die because he wanted to die but because he wanted to live." Now I don't think that says everything about the identity of Christ—no theology does—but it says something. Jesus didn't die because he wanted to die but because he wanted to live fully and freely in God, and the cross was the result.

Jesus' captors did not diminish the value of his engaging with men and women based in love rather than on how networked they were in power. The cross didn't stop the ushering in of the reign. The love and compassion of Christ were even more intensely revealed on the cross. However, at this point I still don't hear trumpets. Injustice had its hour. Jesus was violated, and it was profoundly wrong. And now his resistance is complete. It is finished.

Completion

It is finished. What does Jesus mean? What is finished? Surely not his life—at least not quite. John 19:29 provides yet two more active verbs, with Jesus the living/dying subject of both. Therefore, "It is finished," cannot in any technical sense refer his biological life: he has yet to (a) bow his head, and (b) give up the spirit. On these terms, when Jesus says, "It is finished," his life is not yet done. He is not yet all dead—not completely dead—but mostly dead, with two acts yet to accomplish.

Yet, something "is finished," or "done," or "accomplished," or "completed." Something is over, even if Jesus is not. And that something has to do with his purpose—what he came to accomplish, the race he came to run, the work he came to do, the will he was born to obey.

In John 4:34, Jesus had said, "My food is doing the will of him who sent me, and I will finish his work." In the tenth chapter of John, the Good Shepherd says, "For this reason the Father loves me, because I lay down my life, that I may take it again. No one takes it from me, but I lay it down of my own accord."

Now, in this 19th chapter, in his account of the crucifixion, John tells us, "Therefore, when he had received the sour wine, Jesus said, 'It is finished,' and he bowed his head and gave up the spirit." If doing the work of the One who sent him is, in some sense, Christ's food; and if indeed he has the power to lay down his life—and take it up again, then what Jesus has finished, what he has completed is none other than the Father's saving work, the Father's eternal will, the Father's incomprehensible desire to exchange the life of his only Son for the salvation of the whole inhabited world: the life of One in exchange for the lives of all, the embrace of death for the sake of life.

The fulfillment of this extravagant inequity, the accomplishment of this great work, frees Jesus to announce the completion of his mission, bow his head, and hand over his spirit—not (it might appear) as some failed visionary—not (it might appear) as some pathetic victim—not (it might appear) as an inept guru—but rather to bow his head and hand over his spirit as when the conductor takes a bow; as one satisfied with his work, having completed his task, and now ready to rest from his labors. As when taking a nap, Jesus bows his head and takes a well-earned rest. By his particular death, Christ Jesus transforms death in general into a nap in particular, a sleep, a rest.

This is the goodness of Good Friday: not the violence and misery of suffering and death; but the transformation of all death by means of One death. The obedience of the Son completes the Father's will and accomplishes all things for our salvation. The Spirit beckons us believe it. There can be nothing more. There can be nothing less. It is finished. For our sake, and for all.

The Seventh Word from the Cross

It was now about noon, and darkness came over the whole land until three in the afternoon, while the sun's light failed; and the curtain of the temple was torn in two. Then Jesus, crying with a loud voice, said, 'Father, into your hands I commend my spirit.' Having said this, he breathed his last. Luke 23:44-46

Prayer

Lord Jesus Christ, by your death you have taken away the sting of death. Grant unto us your servants so to follow in faith where you have first led the way, that at length we may commend our spirit into the waiting hands of God, fall peacefully asleep in you, and at your call rise to live and serve you in all eternity—you who abide with the Father and the Spirit, now and forever. Amen.

A Broad place

In the span of three hours, about the time that we have been gathered together here, Luke brings together the upheaval of the universe and the whispers of a dying adult to his father. Through these seemingly opposing events—one so large that our imagination struggles to hold on to it; the other so intimately painful our heart can scarcely bear it— Luke give us the last word from Jesus.

We are at the hour of deepest darkness, when it seems that evil will have its way with the world. Luke's gospel has prepared us for this moment: Jesus says, "Let these words sink into your ears: The Son of Man is going to be betrayed into human hands." Later he says the Son of Man "will be mocked and insulted and spat upon. After they flog him, they will kill him..." But I also see in this dark hour the first birth pangs of a new creation.

To be sure, there is an apocalyptic story unfolding. The darkness and gloom of so many prophets are held together in Luke. But the last word from the cross is cloaked in a pattern of speech that reminds me of Genesis, when we are told of God's creative work, followed by the marking of time: "there was evening, and there was morning, the first day." On this day, in Luke's gospel, time marks the unraveling of creation.

"It was now about noon, and darkness came over the whole land." In Genesis, out of darkness God gathered the waters together and let dry land appear. God let the earth bring forth creatures of every kind, and humankind in God's image. But now on that dry land all is dark again. One man hangs between two others.

At three in the afternoon, the sun's light fails. The curtain of the temple is torn in two, laying bare the holy of holies for all the world, filled with its sin and filth, to see. Here we are, God, just look what we are capable of doing! It is your son, dying on a piece of wood.

The curtain is not lifted gracefully to invite God's people into a new creation, it is cut in half. All of its fine linen threads, blue, purple, and crimson, which had been carefully twisted, skillfully woven, painstakingly preserved for the means to worship God, is broken, severed, torn apart. Jesus says in Luke's gospel, "Do you think that I have come to bring peace to the earth? No, I tell you, but rather division!"

What happens before three o'clock, and what happens after it is finished, changes everything. There was creation before noon, creation given grace to abide in covenant love with God, but a creation steeped in its own desires, its grand plans. And there is creation after three o'clock: creation pulled in deeply to an embrace of love so complicated, so mysterious, that we gather here year after year to wonder and gaze at the cross, at our dying Lord, knowing we are as far from understanding as we were when we took our first breath.

From cosmic darkness and destruction, Luke's gospel invites us into the most intimate of space. We hear words spoken from a dying child to his father. It is not the order of things. It is the ultimate unraveling of creation. Though Jesus was a grown man who had withstood betrayal and denial, taunting and torturing, at this moment before his death he still bears the body of the child we welcomed at Christmas.

The words come to him from Psalm 31. It is the prayer of someone surrounded by hatred, someone who is sure his enemies are about to kill him. The certainty of death is no less after this surrender—after all, we are all dust. Yet, the psalmist finds hope that this is not his time. He trusts that God will lift him out of the hands plotting to take his life and into God's hands, where he will be given a broad place to live. This word translated, "a broad place", a "Rehoboth", also takes us back to Genesis. It is the name for the spot where Isaac found a water well, where he finally knew that he could settle, that God had made room for him.

Like the psalmist, Jesus commends his spirit to God, but it does not follow as in the psalm. It is his time. Jesus is not delivered from the hand of the enemy, his feet are not set in a broad place. His feet are resting on nothing but a nail.

But what Jesus finished on the cross means that there is a broad place, there is room for us, there is a kingdom into which we are welcome to come. Jesus had nowhere to stand so that we could stand together with God's creation and worship God without the fear of death. And we have every reason to fear: darkness and gloom surround us. For some of us, every day feels like noon on Good Friday. When guilt consumes us. When loneliness is our nearest friend. When our bodies fail. When children die before their parents. We live in the new creation given to us in Jesus Christ, but we experience the pain of a creation still disordered.

This new creation is birthed in death. The last thing we hear from Jesus is a loud cry, "Father, into your hands I commend my spirit." From the cross, the one who was with God in the beginning, who was there when there was nothing but darkness and a formless void, who grieved as we departed the garden, gives his spirit, his lifeblood, his lifes work and now his death, to the very hands that created it all in the first place. And he calls him "Father." He takes up our most deeply held fears, our most vulnerable moments and bears them for us. This last word is the first word of the new creation. And it is a word given to us.

In the new creation we are free to call out to God, in a loud voice or in a quiet murmur, and give our spirit into God's hands. We hope we will be intimate enough with God that these words will be our dying breath. This verse is often included in the Jewish practice of reciting the *Shema* at the end of the day. "Into your hands I commend my spirit." Jewish parents say it to their babies, and it is recited by children as they grow older. Sitting on the edge of the bed, ready to fall into a much-needed sleep, a child commends her spirit to God. For me, this is my airplane prayer. Sitting on the small cushion of 31A or 15C or the many seats in which I have safely sat, I commit myself and those around me, into God's hands.

But God's new creation, accomplished once, for all, is not only for our dying breath. It is not just to fall asleep with and to prepare for take-off. To pour ourselves into God's hands is the gift made possible by this death. It is for life!

Imagine what the church is capable of doing if we commend our spirit, as a whole, to the hands of God. To whom would we be called once our life breath is in God's hands? Could we learn to love our near neighbors more deeply? To seek out distant neighbors and join in mission together? To speak new languages together and taste of the kingdom of God in unexpected ways? What would it be like to make these last words Jesus cries out from the cross to be the first words we speak at the dawn of each day? Father, into your hands I commend my spirit.

A way to die

We are at the end. Jesus had three long hours to die. He spoke to God. He spoke to a thief; he spoke to his family. He spoke to his followers. And now at the very end, he speaks again to the Father. The bible says it is a fearful thing to fall into the hands of the living God. It is a fearful thing to commend one's life to God. Why? Because who knows what God will do with your life. You commend your life to God on a Sunday morning and you may be shocked to find out what God calls you to do or endure on a Monday morning.

Our only reassurance is the promise that God will never allow anything worse to happen to us than he allowed to happen to his own Son. Now doesn't that make you feel better? I think most of us spend most of our lives trying to get our lives out of God's hands and into our own hands. We achieve and we work; we build and we hoard. We work out at the gym and watch our cholesterol. For most of us, if God wants my life, God will have to damn well come and take it. And truth to tell, in the end, one way or another, God does. We die.

"I fled him down the nights and down the days. I fled him down the arches of the years." So says Francis Thompson in the poem, "The Hound of Heaven." Some of you know first hand what it is like to be pursued, stalked, and tracked down by the living God. It is a fearful thing. Well that is not what we are talking about here.

What we are talking about here is one so close, so one with the living God, he could do what we in our poverty could not: namely commend himself and the significance of all he had done, the purpose of his whole life and worth, and the darkness of his death – hand it all over to God. The pursuing God did not have to pursue his own son.

In the early days of the Wesleyan tradition, they witnessed to something they called a happy death. A happy death referred to a death in which the person was so perfected in love, so close to God, that they slipped into death with a joy that comes from a short journey from life to death to God. I fear we have few happy deaths these days. Because most of us, in death, make a very long arduous trip from total self-absorption in this life, to the most anxious and reluctant total loss in our death.

Jesus on the other hand, did not have a very long way to go to get to the Father, since he and the Father are One. So commending his life to the Father, Jesus' last word is a take charge, direct, confident word. "Father, into your hands, I commend my spirit." In the past several hours, Jesus had been arrested, bound, whipped, moved to and fro through the praetorium, humiliated before the crowds, and finally nailed to the cross. And yet, it is precisely at this moment that Jesus takes charge. He takes his life out of the hands of his tormentors and places it confidently in the hands of the Father. He will not let his crucifiers have the last word, to determine the significance of his cross.

It is not news that Jesus is dying. You must die, I must die, all creatures die. And with Jesus, having said the words that he said, and done the things that he had done, you knew he wasn't going to die a natural death. He was going to die and at the hands of those he most offended. It is the way the world treats its prophets and saints, as Jesus himself reminded us. It is not that he died; it is the way that he died. There is a way to die. He is saying to us—they didn't take my life away; I commended my life to the Father.

Saint Paul writes: "He is the image of the invisible God, the firstborn of all creation; for in him all things in heaven and on earth were created, things visible and invisible, whether thrones or dominions or rulers or powers—all things have been created through him and for him. He himself is before all things, and in him all things hold together. He is the head of the body, the church; he is the beginning, the firstborn from the dead, so that he might come to have first place in everything. For in him all the fullness of God was pleased to dwell, and through him God was pleased to reconcile to himself all things, whether on earth or in heaven, by making peace through the blood of his cross."

We are at the end. Here we sit in darkness and silence. The next move will be up to God.

Last words

Last words. Tradition holds them more meaningful than the rest, even inspirational—as though someone's last expression, their final expiration were for those yet alive—a final inspiration, a meaning-full inhalation of another's final exhalation. So from Luther, we inhale, "We are all beggars"; from Thomas Aquinas, we take in, "All my work is straw." Or from the Confederate General T.J. "Stonewall" Jackson, expiring at Chancellorsville, we take in and ponder, "Let us cross the river and rest beneath the shade of the trees." The famous fighting man expiring toward rest. But then T. J. Jackson always did rest at strange and awkward moments—and especially in the midst of battle. While armies raged, he slept; and while others either fled or fought in confusion, he stood like a stone wall. Still, Jesus (himself the rock) exhales neither soldierly valor nor tranquil rest, but childlike obedience to a faithful parent.

Jesus' final words—whether a Psalm of lament (as in Mark and Matthew) or a Psalm of affirmation (as here in Luke)—come from anything but a stone wall. And especially here in Luke, the crucified Messiah prays as an obedient child who, having done his work, having accomplished what he was called to do, commends his spirit—his life breath—into the hands of his father. This word, "father" troubling, perhaps, in an age of abuse—here suggests not one who manipulates, but one who waits and receives what at last is given: father as one who depends on the gift of a child.

"Father, into your hands I commit my spirit." With the exception of "Father," the words quote Psalm 31.5 almost to the letter. The Psalm addresses itself to "O Lord," or "O Lord, God of truth," or "my strong rock," "my crag and my stronghold"—terms of vivid imagery. God as rock, crag, and stronghold communicates protection, security, and rugged defense. Verse 7, however, rejoices in "your steadfast love," a phrase suggestive of a personal relationship between the crucified Jesus and God as "father."

Addressing God as "father," the crucified Jesus employs personal terms, but not as we might. He doesn't call God "Father" to gain any privilege, advantage, or power. We might imagine ourselves at the point of excruciating death, straining desperately to breathe and survive according to the body's natural inclination. I imagine myself in such a state: begging for life, making deals, negotiating a reprieve: "Father, if you'll only get me out of this, I'll live a more faithful life, I'll do anything, be more religious, say my prayers, be more generous, care for my neighbors, be nicer to my wife. I'll even love the church."

Jesus engages in none of this. He asks nothing. He gives everything—even his final breath, his very spirit into the care of a waiting parent—God the Father all-suffering. Christ's final words are not a plea, request, or negotiation. The words reflect simple trust in God as faithful father, one who can be relied on to receive without reservation what Jesus offers. He gives what God is apparently ready and prepared to receive—his life, his spirit, his very being into the Father's control.

The Father sent him for this very purpose: to die on behalf of the whole murderous, faithless, and self-obsessed world. This he has now accomplished and, as such, he has no need of the life-spirit he hands over to the One Person he trusts—the Person of God the Father. Everything is accomplished, and he is now free to give up all for our sake: Father, into your hands I commend my spirit. As he said this, he expired.

Contributors

The Rev. Cindy Crane currently serves as director of the anti-bullying ministry of the South-Central Synod of Wisconsin of the ELCA.

The Rev. Jon Enslin is a retired bishop of the South-Central Synod of Wisconsin of the ELCA.

The Rev. Sherri Frederickson is currently serving the church in North Dakota.

Ms. Amy Grunewald Mattison graduated with a master of divinity degree from Duke University. She currently serves as director of the Luther Memorial Sunday School program.

The Rev. Twink Jan-McMahon currently serves as associate pastor at First United Church of Christ in Fitchburg, Wisconsin.

Ms. Amy Johnson is the former director of the Lutheran Office for Public Policy in Wisconsin and is currently enrolled in law school at Drake University.

The Rev. Jim Koza serves as chaplain at the Skaalen Nursing Home in Stoughton, Wisconsin.

The Rev. Brad Pohlman, editor of this series, is currently the associate pastor of Luther Memorial.

Mr. Dan Ruge graduated with a masters degree from Philadelphia Lutheran Seminary and currently works as a biology researcher.

The Rev. John Ruppenthal is a retired pastor having served several congregations in Wisconsin.

The Rev. Peter Sherven is a retired pastor having served several congregations in Wisconsin.

The Rev. Larry Thies is a retired pastor having served several congregations in Wisconsin.

The Rev. Franklin Wilson is currently the senior pastor of Luther Memorial.

www.ingramcontent.com/pod-product-compliance
Lightning Source LLC
Chambersburg PA
CBHW070106100426
42743CB00012B/2656